Vine

Other books by Melody Lee

Moon Gypsy, A Collection of Poetry and Prose

Vine

Book of Poetry

Melody Lee

Vine: Book of Poetry

Copyright © 2018 Melody Lee
Wild Orchid Publishing
Florida / USA

First Edition
All rights reserved.

ISBN 978-0-692-12721-6
Library of Congress Control Number: 2018906243

Cover and book design by Sarah E. Holroyd
            (https://sleepingcatbooks.com)
Editor: Christina Strigas

For Colby and Dallas

Table of Contents

Foreword

When Melody approached me about writing the foreword to her second collection of poetry, I was absolutely honored. Melody and I have been friends now for about a year, but it feels like much longer than that. Our mutual love for poetry gave us a common ground, but it was her charisma and kindness that created a life-long bond of friendship. She is the kind of person that you can instantly connect with because of her inviting personality, and that skill reflects in her poetry.

She is a passionate writer and friend, and her fire for writing shines through every piece of poetry and prose that she creates, leaving us feeling warmer from having read it, while also lighting fires within our own hearts to live fulfilling and meaningful lives.

In her second poetry collection, Melody Lee builds upon the poetic voice we have all come to love, while also evolving in *Vine: Book of Poetry* with increased focus on fantasy, inspiration, and passion.

The book is divided into sections of vines: clematis, honeysuckle, jasmine, poison ivy, and wisteria. The garden that she has created focuses on the different emotions that each symbol evokes in the reader: strength, happiness, love and sensuality, soul-searching, and perseverance in the face of adversity.

The imagery and use of fantasy flawlessly weaves each topic together with the underlying theme of nature enduring through each section. I love the way she divided this collection into sections based on different types of vines because it plays so perfectly into the mystical and magical theme woven through the book's pages. Each section opens with a brief description of why the specific vine was chosen, and we can all find elements of each vine of nature that we feel describes our personalities or our current situations.

Melody uses nature as a profound tool in her poetry, drawing parallels to our experiences and the beauty of the world around us. It's a very empowering thing to be able to relate to such breathtaking elements of nature, and I think that her use of vines throughout was a perfect symbol to use as her underlying theme. I love that each "vine" was carefully selected to inhibit certain emotions in the reader, depending on subject matter. It was such a creative way to tie everything together.

"I wake with the taste of poetry on my tongue, sticky on my pillow, as if I dreamt of falling in meandering pastures of honeysuckles." In this poem titled "Honey," Melody writes about her deep appreciation of poetry. Her writing encourages readers to experience the words, as it draws in the senses and immerses you in a world of imagery.

One of the things I love most about this collection is the personal undertones delivered throughout the book. While we have grown to love Melody through *Moon Gypsy*, this collection gives us an additional personal touch. She discusses some of her favorite things: Frankenstein, Edgar Allen Poe, gothic corsets, and the color purple. She discusses some of her personal experiences with heartbreak and falling in love. Her words are so relatable while also giving you an exclusive look into what makes her who she is. It takes a talented writer to be able to combine the personal and the relatable in such a seamless way.

Melody knows her readers and provides us all with a safe haven in her words. Her work gives us a chance to press pause on the chaos of our lives and get lost in her mythical and enchanting world of words. When you start reading, you are immediately transported to the garden of her soul, where you get to take a tour of all the different plants that grow there and find the ones that resonate with you and your personal story.

Another thing I love about Melody's writing is the wisdom she shares with us throughout the collection. She discusses the importance of discovering ourselves on our journey to happiness. She supports the empowerment of self and our fellow women. And, she gives some incredible life advice about not falling prey to the money trap or worrying too much about what others think of us. Her writing is an inspiring world of fantasy and also a relatable sphere of real-life advice that we can implement into our day-to-day when we have to return from our journey to Melody's beautiful realm of imagery.

An excerpt from her poem "Sages" reads: "You'll only find your extraordinary wings when you let go of hate and greed and material things. Oh, those old artistic souls with poets' hearts and gypsy blood. Like wise old sages: They know, they know, they know." Melody does a fantastic job of combining elements of fantasy with relatable and personal encounters. She is imaginative and eloquent, a superb story-teller.

Those of us who already love Melody's writing will fall even more in love with her words. And, for those of you who are experiencing Melody's poetry for the first time, prepare to be delighted by *Vine*.

☙ Liz Newman, author *Hope Between Heartbeats*

CHAPTER I

Clematis, Queen of Vines

These extraordinary vines are some of the most beautiful flowering plants, known for blooming lavishly on trellises, fences, and porches. They get larger and stronger every year. Be patient, sometimes they take their time growing. It usually takes about two years for a newly-planted vine to come into its own.

ᖗ Google via American Meadows Inc.

This is How I Know

Madness devours me
Like Plath, Bukowski
Scribbling thoughts erratically
Insanity is ecstasy
Love, it is manic
Brutal, excruciatingly exquisite
Piercing the soul, deeply
Haunting in a heavenly way

Blossoming like tulips in Amsterdam
Dahlias, southern pink magnolias
I spread like a butterfly violet
Under mesmeric caresses
Cascading into white waves
I am the spherical bubbles in champagne
Sparkling, intoxicating
I move mountains and fly above them
I scurry in fields of poppies and dandelions

Becoming love, the unparalleled, transcendental kind
This is how I know, love has enraptured me
It gracefully dances up my spine
Gently wrapping around my heart
And I flourish extravagantly
The way unkempt vines do in their natural habitats
Love has opened a chamber
In the deep well of my soul.

Cunning Linguist

Literature, pure ecstasy
Long ago found its way
Into my bones
And crawled inside the creases
Of my heart
I wear it like luxurious cashmere
I savor the feel of it as I would
Egyptian cotton sheets covering bare skin
Cool sand between my toes or
Snowflakes on my cheeks
Sometimes, I re-visit the classics
Like a horse ridden for relaxation
Or a trail hike for stress relief

Words melt in my heart
Like milk chocolate on my tongue
Sweet and warm in my mouth
Some stick to my skin
Like dirty secrets and sin

Haikus in my head
Lyrics on my lips
I gulp, I sip, swallow
Sonnets in my bed
I write until I bleed
Aphorisms
Idioms
Elegies
Poetry will never be dead

I am a book harlot
I want books, colossal amounts of books
Stories, biographies, folklore
Because I am addicted to words, you see,
They have a grip on me.

Warning

They should have warned you
that little princesses grow up
to be red rocks and raging seas,
fire dragons and warrior queens.

Education

You won't learn about life
Until you experience life—

Get messy
Play in the dirt
Take a few falls, let them happen
Cuts and bruises, scrapes and scars
Are good for the soul –
You bleed, you heal, you rise.

Go places, everywhere you can
See the world—
Bring a journal, a camera
Try new foods
Meet new people, make new friends
Different cultures
Bring you to your authentic self.

Get hobbies
Experiment
Be interested in various things
But stay true to your values
Realize though, as you grow
Those values may change and that is okay
As long as you are following your heart
And not what others want or expect
Because then you are not being true to you.

Keep an open mind—
Let it drift, let it dream
Then let it bring you back to reality.

Mistakes, don't avoid or fear them
In fact, allow and welcome them
They are part of growth
This is how you learn
Fail so you can succeed
Get back up
You'll gain confidence
You'll be proud
And rightly so.

Follow your heart
Never go against what you feel is true
If you hurt someone, apologize
It takes an evolved person to admit defeat
To admit being wrong
Be a big person and you won't go wrong.

Be happy
Shed some tears
Live in a way that you have few regrets.

Find love, fall into it and let it warm you to the bones
Then come back and tell me about life.

This is adventure, this is life
This is education.

Indelible

I was told if I fell in love
with a poet
I would become immortal,
so I decided
to become the poet
and make all those
who touched my soul, eternal.
I write friends and lovers
into my stories,
weaving them into fragments
of sonnets and prose,
the nectar of my poetry.
My muses, perennial…
Evergreen.

Poets

Poets are devils and angels
Lions and lambs
Wild creatures, crescent moons
We are lovers and madmen
Dashing, daring, rebellious and brave
Filled with passion and rage

We are pulsing rivers and ancient forests
Junipers and maple trees
Poets are you and I
Weeping roses, brambles and prickly thorns
Beautifully adorned with words
Resonating truths and fabricated lies

We are like an evocative painting
Intense, seductive, mysterious, brilliant
Majestic landscapes, rugged mountains
And crystalline skies
Loners and misfits, rainbows and fireflies

Poetry, like art, like music, like magic
Lives inside all of us
But poets take the ride on that esoteric carpet
We have discovered our mighty wings
As flawed as they may be
We have discovered how to fly

Poetry is reality and fantasy in a pretty package
It doesn't always have to make sense
It just has to make magic.

You

I keep stars in my pockets
wear daisies in my hair
but I tuck you tenderly
in the folds of my heart
and take you everywhere.

Are You Ready?

I am ready to abandon fear
to tread the unknown path
the uncertainty, the mystery
the joy of discovering more
of the world, internal riches
more of you.
Are you ready to wander with me
to take my hand
to stumble, to dance
to rocket to the moon?
Are you ready to embrace
the unknown and fly into ecstasy?
Ready to get completely lost in love with me?

*Let's jump in the rabbit hole, ditch our fears,
and watch, like magic, how strength appears.*

Traveling

It is beautiful when
you allow your mind
to wander
to places it has never been—

imagination
crawling, curling, twisting
as vines left to their natural tendencies
lovers loving
intoxicated in dreams—

write about it
to experience the euphoria
of traveling
to those places
all over again.

*Drunk on imagination,
that's my kind of intoxication.*

Tempest

She's wild like whiskey
and fierce like the sea.
She belongs to no one,
yet, she belongs willingly,
so completely to me.

Coffee

Pour yourself a cup of steaming coffee,
honey, then come pour yourself into me.
I need you like you need your morning fix.
You need me to breathe.
And today, I need you to love me
like the moon loves the fearless sea.
Love is the only thing
that will heal our tormented hearts.
Love is the only thing that will set us free.

Remember that misty night years ago
when we embraced under the September sky?
We ate fresh peaches and drank too much Sangria.
We talked about music, religion and philosophy.
We spoke of road trips and made plans
to hike the Appalachian Trails.
You told me how your best friend survived a bear attack.
I caught a chill, you pulled me into your chest.
I heard your heart singing and it sounded
like Beethoven's Fifth Symphony.
You smelled of manly confidence, quite an aphrodisiac.
You have always been my favorite scent.

Suddenly, two shooting stars collided.
Our souls merged.
You pulled me close, cupping my face tenderly
with your beautiful hands
tracing the outline of my cracked lips
with your fingertips.

You kissed me for the first time. It was perfect.
I fell in love with you that night.
This was how love was supposed to feel, invincible.
We fell asleep arm in arm, cheek to cheek
under a canopy of shooting stars.
In the morning you made coffee
and we made love.
We were captivating to each other.
We were completely free.

Let's Be Honest

Let's be honest…
We are frantic, fervent lovers,
devoted to each other.
We argue, we fight…we disagree,
but we worship each other
on skin and dirty knees,
with unforgettable kisses and undeniable pleas.

You beguile me. I bewitch you.
We are tumultuous—our color is fire,
our sign is pandemonium. We are intricate together—
best when we are connected as one,
yet still separate beings.

Our love is made of multifarious components.
Our love is tougher than bone,
hard to break, impossible to bend.
Devout and devoted, we no longer have a beginning.
And we certainly have no end. We are sacred.

You Are So Much More

Some days she is delicate,
vulnerable and soft.
Other days she is a lioness;
courageous, determined, unafraid.
Always she is a goddess,
a tenacious warrior's heart.
She is you, him and her.
No one is without flaws,
yet we are all flawless.
Quite the contraction,
still, so very true.
Never underestimate your worth
your beauty or your strength.
You are everything you can imagine
and so much more.

Stumbalina

I am the girl that goes backwards,
takes wrong turns,
stumbles in life's chasms.
I am also the girl that finds gold
where others feared to stray.
Perhaps because I follow my heart,
instead of sage advice thrown my way.
I do not want to become numb
by always playing it safe;
not hiking that eleven-mile trail up rugged terrain,
traveling to a writer's convention across the globe,
or taking on a chance on love.
Many of our most cherished times happen
when we shatter our own-inflicting cages,
smash confining boxes,
jump in ravines,
take chances,
listen to the sound of our soul,
and follow our dreams.

Right turns

on wrong days,
one of life's
many conundrums.

Jewels

People will come
People will go
Who cares
If you do, don't
Treasures stay
Trash goes
You've got style
Polychromatic mind
Kaleidoscopic art
Some people
Cannot handle
Such brilliance
The luster too much
For their tiny eyes
And shallow souls.

Luminosity

Be patient my little wild one,
wondrous things take time.
A pearl is hidden before it's refined.
A diamond's luster is dull before revealing brilliant
magnificent breathtaking shine.

Perception

Where you see scars
I see art
Where you see flaws
I see incredible beauty
Where you see failures
I see knowledge and growth
Everything is perception
You see with your eyes
I see with my soul
It's how you rock
And how I roll.

Garden of Your Soul

Work on yourself—
Feed your mind
Nourish your soul
Find your passion;
Water it, nurture it
Let it take root and blossom
Let yourself be consumed
Let yourself drown in what you love
Open your heart, also guard it
Love your body
Be wild but wise
Be soft not fragile
Sensitive not weak
Strong not hard
Humble not meek
Be kind. Be love
Be raw and real
Fill your life with adventures
Include quiet and soulful things
Make memories, lots of them
Rid yourself of negative thoughts
Toxic people, excess stress
Do all of the above, continuously, every day
Add to this list as you see fit, but don't
Complicate your life with unnecessary "things" and "its"
This is how you heal and grow
This how you tend the garden of your soul.

*You've got to plant flowers in the center
of your soul if you want to bloom.*

Unshakable

You are thunder and lightning
Love and rage
Intensity and sensitivity
Made of mountains, oceans
Fire and fierce things
Dreams and curiosity
You are paradoxes and contradictions
Some days soft, some days
Strong as fuck
Always beautiful.

War and Peace

The mind and the heart are at constant odds with each other—war and peace—the internal struggle. While the mind wants to pick up a sword and go to battle, the heart wants to offer compassion and make love. This is why I prefer following the beats of my heart. I like making love more than I like making war.

Patchworks of Poetry

Stories I read and people I love,
conversations I have had, dreams
I've lost and found, these all become
part of me, embedded in my DNA,
and if they are lucky, eventually,
these things I cherish will be
stitched into patchworks of poetry.

First Impressions

Shiny, perfect things
Expensive cars, fancy diamond rings
Hardly impress me
Rather mundane, shallow, uninspiring
Give me rough around the edges any day
Dreadlocks and tousled hair are fine by me
Body piercings
Quirky things
Vintage art, old records and books appeal to me
Because they have charm, more personality
I prefer a healthy dose of witty intellect
Tell me of your travels, your adventures
Your favorite authors
Movies and music you love and why
Stimulate my mind with knowledge and insight
Scariest thing you have ever done
Saddest moment of your life
Exhilarating conversations keep me thinking on my feet
Keep reaching for my soul, delve deep
Let us engage our minds
Discover things we didn't know we knew.

Sages

Oh, those old artistic souls
With poets' hearts and gypsy blood
Movers and shakers of the world
Who don't fit in and always stand out
Fluttering among us with words and art
They live in a world colored
With mangoes, oranges and aquamarine
Skies filled with blues, blacks and tangerine
Singing, painting and creating out loud
They belong to nobody and no crowd
Playing only the strings of their serendipitous hearts
Being rebellious as only nonconformists can be
Courageous and brave they love unafraid
They've abandoned conventional society
For peace and love and harmony
Beautiful lovers tangled in dreams
Catching hopeful breezes
Knowing there is a better way
War is not the answer
Fighting doesn't work
Greed robs souls of divinity
Normal doesn't reside in their vocabulary
It's all about the moment—
Being in it, feeling it, touching and tasting it

Those lovers of love—
The bohemian way
The road of genuine joy and riches
Is not accumulating "stuff"

Don't buy into the lie you've been told
Life is about creating and dancing and doing and loving
Life is about adventures
Wealth is a mental attitude, a soulful
Journey, a heart's delight
Expressing passions through movement and musings
Not an abundance of stocks and bonds
Silver and gold and platinum rings
You'll only find your extraordinary wings when you let go
Of hate and greed and material things
Oh, those old artistic souls
With poets' hearts and gypsy blood
Like wise old sages

They know, they know, they know.

Dear Reader

Don't say poetry doesn't make sense
while you are eating the words
as if they are a last meal,
as your backbone curves, as goose bumps
rise on your legs, arms.
That is all the sense poetry needs to make,
that is poetry's intent.
Dear reader, if you feel the writer's words
like a charge of electricity
running up and down your spine
or the tip of a blade grazing your breastbone,
the poet's voice is speaking to you.
If those same words resonate to your core,
poetry is climbing into your soul.
Poetry does not always feel like a pleasant ocean breeze;
it is not always dainty and pretty like pink flamingos
on a sandy beach
or regal like Clydesdales prancing down royal streets.
Sometimes poetry is dark and brutal,
has fangs and teeth.
Sometimes it shudders, sometimes it stings;
that is all the sense poetry needs to make.

CHAPTER II

Honeysuckle

The honeysuckle signifies happiness. Honeysuckle also symbolizes devoted affection in the form of a lover's embrace.

Honeysuckles are heat-tolerant and wildly attractive in any garden. Honeysuckles are great additions to any landscape and will draw abundant wildlife with its sweet, yellow to bright-red blossoms.

∾ Google

Honey

I wake with the taste
of poetry
on my tongue,
sticky on my pillow,
as if I dreamt of falling
in meandering pastures
of honeysuckles.

Crash Landing

You didn't waltz into my life
like Fred Astaire and Ginger Rogers
dancing on air.
Quite the contrary,
you made a crash landing
in the center of my heart,
blazing guns and glory.

I knew you were not the storybook type,
you were my type, eccentric, dreamy,
rebellious motorcycle rider,
and one hell of a hot-blooded man.

You loved Michelangelo and Roman Architecture,
Matisse and Monet.
Handmade antique mahogany bookshelves
housed your collection of art and wildlife books,
when they weren't scattered on the floor
near our naked bodies.

You were ambitious in your pursuit
of painting murals across Europe
and the South Atlantic.
I always loved that contrast.
I always loved the romantic genius in you.

Perfectly off balance, like me.
Scintillating like the sun,
vast and luminous like the sky,

mysterious and elusive like the night,
you were exactly my type.

Dark Purity

He has dirty hands
and dark wild eyes, but
by far he is the purest
heart I have ever known.
*My eyes saw you, but damn,
did my soul feel you.*

Animal Magnetism

Wavy hair
reckless eyes
an aura quite magnetic
can't help but stare
I am mesmerized
as in a daydream
romantic serenity
has captured me.

I want your lips
upon my mouth
to breathe you in
and keep you there
to sink my teeth
into your skin
to feel your soul
and taste your mind
am I staggering?
I feel drunk.

But please...
do not wake me up
I like this reverie
trance-like state
daring me
to submerge deep
inside your dark
enchanting
dangerous eyes.

For Keeps

I'll be your poet
if you'll be my muse
strum your guitar
I'll write you some blues
make love to my mind, go real deep
I'll kiss your soul and steal your heart
you'll fall in-love, I'll be yours forever, for keeps.

Little Black Dresses

What is it about those little black dresses?
Don't girls wear scarlet or witchcraft anymore?
Black has become the new white
and I desire purple, fire and wine,
taut around my waist, loose on my skin,
caressing my breasts, my supple flesh.

Wicked Feeding

You were a ravenous one
a surreptitious feline feeding
on broken hearts
yet loving unconditionally
nothing could tear you apart
from true love's appetite
such wicked delight.

And, there she appeared
a lunatic under your thumb
ensnared in your web
transfixed in your spell
impish, savage
perfect for the hungry beast in you.

You both were meant to be
to fall in love and feast in lust
the sun may hide, the moon may cry
but certainly, this hunger
will not be denied.

Rapturous

He felt like sin
but tasted like love
so, what's a clumsy girl
to do but stumble in
delicious rapturous love.

Serendipitous Synchronicity

We loved at first sight
yet the world criticized,
condemned us
saying our love could not be so,
love needs time and experience to grow.

It is the world that is blind
to natural organic instantaneous love…
Where the eyes are limited by sight
the soul universally feels far beyond,
just as lovers who feel it like
serendipitous synchronicity.

Love can be enigmatic,
so can Mars and planets
and outer space,
but none of them are less real
in the heart or mind,
whether love happens instantly
or blossoms with time.

Love does not always make perfect sense;
that does not make it any less real,
that does not make it any less ours.

Cosmic Collision

Our souls collided long before we were born
wrapped in human skin. Now, all these
light years later we meet again, this time with eyes
and mouths and flesh and skin. We touch, we kiss,
we laugh, we love. Soul on soul, flesh on flesh.
When we kiss it is as if every language
converges into one universal tongue, and I swear
I hear angels applaud and see the devil smiling.
Galaxies intersect, even heaven and hell unite.
The sun, the stars, the moon, oh how we mesh, we do!

Nothing Less

Possess me with your love
Wholly, completely, devour me
Call me selfish, this is how I demand my lovers
Soul on soul, flesh on flesh, nothing less
A feverish kind of love
Fire and storm
Wild and calm
Gentle and strong
The forever kind
Bring me to the nape of your neck
Wrap me inside the crevices of your heart
Hold me close, never part
We shall love eternally, like Annabel Lee
in the castle by the sea
And Count Dracula, in the dark chambers
of immortality
Your heart and soul and mind I shall possess
Greedily, hungrily, as ferocious lovers do.

La Petite Mort

Take me to that special place
where you kiss me
and the world forgets to exist
fears evaporate
insecurities obliterate.

There is hungry desperation
in a lover's kiss
when it is enamored in love
and I am famished for the depth
of your soul
your body's intoxicating embrace.
My longing is excruciating enough
to make this strong woman weak
this sane woman go mad.

So, again I beg…
Take me to that special place
where the sea becomes the sky
where day fades into night
so easily when we kiss.

You are so afraid
I might love you to death.
A lovely fear to have.
A legitimate one, too.
La Petite Mort.

Stars and Skin

She's all stars and porcelain skin
velvety petals, purple linen
on warm spring nights
she writes elaborate love letters, the scarlet kind
and reads illicit bedtime stories
under a canopy
of plush palmetto trees
as pretty little moonflowers
sparkle between fleshy bosom
and damp thighs.

Heartstrings

To be worthy of her love,
you must first trace the tip of her soul.

There were many who charmed her,
but only one who truly understood
her mind, graced her heart,
and made her feel deliciously delirious.
When that lovely soul kissed her soul,
her heart became a thousand times more beautiful.

Their romance began when she shared
with him her love of
Henry Miller and Anais Nin—the books, the diaries,
the letters between the two Paris lovers,
the movie, "Henry and June."
Their connection was strong, immediate.
It did not take long for love to flourish.

How many times did they watch Moulin Rouge
and cry at the end? Every single time.
They often disagreed tumultuously
like Noah and Allie in 'The Notebook,'
but the amorous love imbued for each other,
the "can't breathe without you" kind of love
was the kind of love they personified.
It was a tempestuous affair,
at times, even, like Scarlett and Rhett,
always like Tristan and Isolde,
immortal lovers traveling
through space and time.

Drowning in Beautiful Intricacies

Those things that take my breath away—
lush Japanese gardens, Polynesian mountains
gushing crystal waterfalls, pastel sunsets painted
over cerulean skies—
become the ocean, complex and deep,
gripping my throat, transfixing my soul,

and I am prone to drowning in rivers
of strange, beautiful intricacies
like the concaves of your opulent soul,
freckles painted on your cheeks like tiny wildflowers,
and cute button nose,
your flaming red hair and pouty lower lip,
captivating essence and smooth swaying hips.
How I could not get lost in thoughts
of your luscious kiss?

Then you look at me
with those inquisitive eyes,
large emeralds of the sea permeating me.
No words spoken, yet I am hypnotized.
I have always been a meticulous climber...
This time I will fall and crash,
and I have always been an excellent swimmer,
now I'm sinking, I am sure of it.

Dirty Sweet Symphony

I
like
when
your
mind
plays
with
mine.
We
harmonize
like
a
dirty
sweet
symphony.

Garden in My Heart

Your love pours warm,
like an afternoon Jamaican rainfall
in the vascular bundle of
my oxygen-depleted veins,
growing like a Wonderland,
a wild garden in my heart.
Your love feels like a fresh start
and tastes like I want forever with you.

*You put butterflies back into my soul
and painted their wings with passion and poetry.*

Twin Flames

I loved him because the crazy
in his heart only wanted me.
He didn't care
what others thought.
I was the one
who aroused his senses
and understood the turmoil of his mind.

I was not afraid of his darkness,
the Friesian horse residing within,
and that terrified, yet comforted him.
I craved his hell
to feel life again.
He needed my tranquility
to soothe his inner turmoil.

We were a mystical balancing act
of equilibrium. Two precious wild hearts
syncing together the way twin flames sometimes do,
interlacing like two aerial artists
pirouetting in the clouds,
converging as one.

CHAPTER III

Jasmine

Jasmine is associated with love. Also symbolizes beauty and sensuality. In some cultures, Jasmine represents appreciation and good luck. When used in religious ceremonies jasmine represents purity.

∾ Wikipedia

Jasmine

The smell of your lust
like marmalade
burning incense
oranges and jasmine
difficult to resist.

The Story of Us

"Why do you love me," she asked. "Because you are the light and I am the moth. You can't control your flame and I damn sure cannot control my attraction to it. You are going to rise for all your goodness and I will smolder in hell for causing you harm and breaking your heart," he replied.

As his sable eyes began to well up and his long lashes became wet with salty tears, she reached over to cradle him in her ethereal embrace. She wiped his wet, chiseled cheeks. Their eyes met, their souls locked, you could feel heat as the love between them caught fire as an explosion of two souls bursting in the atmosphere.

Some blazes can't be extinguished; some forces can't be controlled. And I will love you whether you want me to or not. There is no other way for me to exist without love, the soul bursting, heart-exploding kind of powerful magnetic love we crave.

That is what you have with me, that's what we share. You can no more diminish that radiance than I can make the earth stop revolving.

Full Throttle Love

There are no brakes in loving you.
No life preservers. It is full throttle
or nothing at all. I cannot stop, I won't stop.
I will drown in love and return dripping
with madness and poetry.
It is an art, a gift, this kind of lunacy.

Beautiful Catastrophe

Sometimes I find myself
in the eye of my own hurricane.
…He was trouble in my life
interrupting my world
crashing into my dreams
but I was a fucking storm
the lightening to his thunder
so, what more could a little chaos
add but a beautiful catastrophic eruption.

Avant-garde

Sometimes she's the gentle rain caressing you softly
Sometimes she's the hurricane loving you madly

She is a lamb, she is a lion
She's a bird without an aviary

She's not defined as this or that
She is a woman with multifarious colors

She wears many peculiar, breathtaking hats
She is the forest and the fire

The sea and the sun
She is restless and settled

She looks to the stars
Dreams of the moon

Her feet firmly planted to the ground
An avant-garde poet; her uninhibited poem

The gypsy lover and the bohemian muse
She fits in no one's box but her own.

Raincloud

Today, an overload of winter
and gray
my head, pounding
my heart, breaking
those brutal goodbyes
of finality, like death.
Repugnant words from a lover
cannot be undone
their intent is to inflict suffering.
All day
I stay in bed
numbing the pain away
with stale coffee
trashy books
runny ink
whilst the rain pours down
hard in my life and on my heart.
This too shall pass
or so they say.

Dagger

You were a storm I chased
to get my kicks and have some fun;
it backfired when I crashed hard in love.

You were nothing more than a heavy cloud,
a nasty pill that fucked with my head,
your love a bitter tonic
I will pour down the drain
and flush into the sewer.

Today I pulled out the dagger
you lodged in my heart
and scattered your ashes of lies
and repugnancy into the wind.

As I looked up to the sky, suddenly clear,
I screamed from the top
of my lungs, "the end!"
I am repulsed and ashamed.
You are one storm I will never chase again.

Sensual Assault

She was quite unusual—
a harem of ravens and doves
a gallery of exotic art
delightfully complicated
lovely, intriguing
like Eve in the Garden of Eden
dark and divine
she indeed opened my mind
learning about her was a violent awakening
loving her was an exquisite assault of the senses
like cayenne pepper and cinnamon
fireball whiskey and gin
she was hot, tart, inebriating
something you do not forget
like your favorite song
or your first kiss
the way you she made you
feel pleasure and pain
one couldn't help inhaling her soul
memorizing her skin
her dark eyelashes and perfect toes
she was sensual and seductive
Claire du Lune and Fur Elise
wrapped in a crimson kiss.

Peculiar Girl

I enjoy strange and unusual things—
fire eaters with flaming lips,
aerial silk artists who spin musical webs,
tattoos and bearded men.
My spirit desires the bizarre;
bed of nails, cat with two tails.
I am weird like that.
Believe me when I confess
I am comfortable with the madness in you.
Your random 4 a.m. epiphanies,
tsunami of inspiration wakeup calls
are sunbursts of my day!
Your theater of the macabre style
reflects the freakish in me,
this girl with belly button piercings
and gothic corsets,
who loves Zen Arts and Cirque du Soleil,
Martha Graham, mother of modern dance,
Frankenstein and Edgar Allan Poe.
I am the Red Riding Hood who
jaunts bareback on big bad wolves.
Certainly not Snow White
I am more the freaky girl type.

Paradox

You are the calmest, fiercest person I know,
that is enough to lure me into your world
and seduce me into your heart. I have always
enjoyed a good paradox and puzzle.
You are no exception. Like a riddle
I am trying to solve, the challenge
excites me. You intrigue me.
If you step too close, I might even trip
into the maze of your spine, get lodged
in your joints and stuck in your bones.

I love the mystery of you.
Wonder if I would love the reality, too.

Fevered Fantasy

You were nothing more
than a duplicitous fairytale.
Once upon a time,
you were my dashing nightingale
singing songs of eternal love,
and I, your enchanting belle.

I stored our memories
in my collection of short stories,
made you immortal
like a bloodsucking dragon,
a Vampire Lestat.

Sometimes I smile,
whispering your name
where we used to meet
near the edge of the seashore,
always on the cliff of twilight,
where the ocean held your gaze
and the darkness stole your heart.

Our love wasn't all heaven,
we made plenty of hell—
we may even meet there someday,
our lovely fevered fantasy.

Purge

It's 2 a.m.
I'm up with the stars
chatting with the moon again
dripping blood from my poet's pen
purging memories of him
seeking solace
the way wordsmiths do...
frantically
   desperately
     insanely
love never dies gracefully.

Haunting

You come to me at random times
the subliminal message
darting through my mind
the shadow in every corner
a ghost in the night
haunting my heart
ripping me apart
putting another crimp in my life.

You are the fabric twisting
through my subconscious
the dream waking me with a startle
reminding me of your presence
even during sleep.

That is the thing about love
it never leaves
even when it goes
the soul of love
forever haunts
feelings left unsaid
memories taunt
unfinished projects
no final goodbye.

Love Disease

You are the one addiction
I can't quite shake.
You stimulate my mind
and increase my heart rate.

I thought I was strong,
yet you make my body
warm and wild
like a hot spring in Bali
and a tiger in heat.

You make my soul quiver.
When you part
my flesh aches.

The will power I once had is gone
I am easy to sway
to your heart's persuasions
when I turn off my brain
and allow love to lead the way.

Holding out your hand
you gently command me
to be vulnerable, to trust you.
All I want is you, every bit of you
to take me away
to our own special land
of wonderful enchantment
where only you and I exist.

If love doesn't both weaken and strengthen
us simultaneously, we are doing it wrong.

Magical Habits

All addictions aren't bad—
long walks under the stars,
getting lost in your lover's eyes,
kissing your favorite person in the world,
soulful conversations and laughing with friends,
words, books, poetry.
I am an addict of these magical things,
not ashamed to say, I would have it no other way.

Heart Path

They told me to pay attention
to my heart; that it would lead
me to my purpose, my passion.
So, I did, I listened closely
to the timbre of my heart
and it always brought me back to you.

Wild Love

She is wild love
eternal fire—
a sensual blend
of gentle heart
burning desire.
Yes, an acquired taste,
but the truth is once
you fall in love with her,
you'll never recover.
Her love will seep
into your veins like Mozart
and morphine,
you'll never be the same.

Conversation

I read a claim that love is not magic.
Oh, I disagree.
Allow me to explain how magical love can be.

He and I conversed with our eyes.
No words uttered,
yet I felt him
permeating intensely
the way Vivaldi's *Four Seasons*
permeates in my bloodstream
every damn time I hear it.

Electric interaction
arose from our skin.
I was learning him,
he was discovering me.
We became vulnerable with each other,
still, not one word uttered.

This is intimacy becoming magnetic.
This is the kind of closeness I crave—
this peaceful energy, vitality, life-force, electricity;
this is how it feels to fall in love.
Love is magic indeed.

All of You

All I want
is a cabin
in the mountains
a villa on the moon
warm cuddles
and coffee
in the morning
writing until noon
long walks
in the woods
all of you.

Chapter IV

Ivy

Ivy represents the wandering of the soul in its search for enlightenment and it carries a warning to be sure of the direction of your desires so that you avoid being ensnared. All parts of the ivy plant are poisonous if ingested.

Ivy, an evergreen plant, represents eternity, fidelity, and strong affectionate attachment, such as wedded love and friendship. The ivy plant is also a strong plant which can grow in the hardest environment. Another association of Ivy as an evergreen, is perennial life and immortality.

∾ The Goddess Tree via Google

> "Oh roses for the flush of youth,
> And laurel for the perfect prime;
> But pick an ivy branch for me
> Grown old before my time."

Christina Georgina Rossetti

Incorporeal

Your crown is invisible to those
who only look with their eyes.
Search with your soul, if you can—
It is there where you will find
ethereal robes of divinity;
this kind of royalty is incorporeal,
not seen with human eyes
but felt in the aura, the energy
of your being.
The empath in you
will recognize a beautiful soul when you feel one.
So, close your eyes, let yourself
transcend to an infinite world—
This is where you begin
and where you end—
Where there is no beginning and no end...

Church

You are so churchy and cute
with your big fake smile,
frilly sundress.
I tried for a while to be like you,
longer than I care to admit.
Truth is, I am allergic to hypocrites,
the holier than thou type.
I start to itch,
the fight or flight in me gets fidgety as shit.
You see, I am quite flawed, a sinner,
but I am content.
Don't care for neat boxes
where everyone is supposed to conform to fit
or Sunday best, when I am more comfortable being me,
my best everyday not just on a "holy" day.

Those long drawn out sermons screwed with my head,
not the passages read from Holy Scriptures,
but man's interpretations and condemnations.
If Jesus and His apostles were here,
surely, they would be rolling their eyes,
maybe even tipping over tables,
if you would even allow them and their dirty feet
into your spotless, sterile sanctuaries.

At least there were hymns, glorious music, I could enjoy,
At least there was that when I went to church.
Hallelujah! Praise the Lord!

Failed Attempt

If you hear sounds
coming from my chest—
howling, screeching,
flapping, moaning—
it is only the wolf
you tried to trap,
the lark you tried to ensnare,
the woman you tried to tame.
They are all inside me,
roaming freely in my soul,
living wild in my heart,
they can't be chained.

You can chain the dragon,
but you'll never tame the beast.

Badass

Don't think for one second
you can't be anything you want to be—
a warrior, a goddess, a queen-bee.
That is precisely your problem,
you simply don't realize how amazingly brilliant you are.
Your fears only have as much power as you allow.
Relinquish them.
Your potential is only limited by your mind.
In a world that often tries to kill passions,
ignite as resplendent flames.
Rise above complacency and indifference.
Be unshakable in your convictions.
Be persistent in your pursuits.
Keep an open and humble spirit,
rebirthing continuously and as necessary.
Never allow the world to stifle your valiant spirit.
You are a powerful force in a universe
that desperately needs heroes.
Be loyal to your heart, faithful to your causes.
Dazzle the world with charm and grace.
You are badass because you have the power
to embody those heroic qualities.

Angelic Woman

She is kind
quilted in compassion
draped in love
a softness as beautiful and graceful
as swans on a lake
but do not underestimate
her strength—she is fearless
like Joan of Arc
fierce and feisty like Mae West
and as timeless as Cleopatra.

Black Lace Gloves

She twirls like a ballerina
on windmill sails
running barefoot
wherever she desires.
She wears black lace gloves
in sumptuous summer time.
That girl is part wolf, part gypsy child,
the embodiment of bohemian love.
Free spirit winds caress her hair,
scents of wild and earth permeating the air.
She is the girl wearing black lace gloves.

True Story

A man once said,

"Women are like roads, the more curves, the more fun, exciting and dangerous they are."

While the evolved man smiled with class and confidence and said,

"Women with more curves, twists and turns in their minds are the most beautiful, exciting, dangerous creatures alive."

And the evolved woman will accept no less than the evolved man; a man with honor, dignity and depth.

This piece was written by a woman with plenty of curves, both inside and out. This woman is me.

What a shame for shallow men who have difficulty seeing beyond physical appearance, into something deeper than superficial curves.

Your body captured my attention,
but it was your soul that held my gaze.

Doomed

We were doomed
from the start
deceptions
daggers of deceit
slicing my skin
again and again
the blades you
wedged in my heart
every time I let you back in—
thought you could be trusted.
You will forever be an abhorrent taste
in my mouth
swine in the mud
a toad squirming
in my thoughts
never the fragrant flowery poem
I had hoped to write about us.
You are now an elegy in my diary
I keep near my four poster bed
as a reminder that our disastrous love is dead
no longer living, moving
bleeding beautifully in my veins
as you once did.

Sacred and Unbreakable

When catastrophe strikes
compassion and love unite.
A storm cannot break the spirit of love.
A storm may crack your windows,
tear off your roof, wreck your house,
but it absolutely cannot destroy
the foundation you hold within yourself.
Stay strong. Stay rooted.
Carry love in your heart, always,
and know the sacred things in life can't be touched.

Hunger

I like the leopard
in your eyes,
the way they
turn feral,
dangerous
when I am near.
Nebula floating
making me high.
And the heat
from your stalwart bones
when you brush
against my silky skin.
I feed on that animal,
I am famished again.
Come here, my lover,
my confidant,
my best friend.
Let us indulge on the temples
of each other
and get full on unbridled love.

Cosmic Intercourse

His eyes were the sea;
gentle and vast,
turbulent,
crashing exuberant waves
into her immaculate heart.

Her eyes;
girlish, seraphic, catlike,
a haunting shade of jade,
celestial, bewitching,
filled of holy, midnight, mystery.

Together they collided;
planetary explosions,
souls entwining, eternity unfolding.

Forbidden Things

Forbidden things—
my God, I'm drawn
to them like a moth
to a flame.

Italian Sonnet

Your parting lips
your hungry mouth
your teasing tongue
taste of eloquent lyrics
and lusty love letters
wanton desire blooms inside me
and I feel like James Joyce's
"dark-blue rain-drenched flower"
you bewitch me, a combination
of chivalry and obscenity
you feel like sensual art
sleek, like Degas's painted dancers
and Picasso's "Blue Nude"
sculpted like Donatello's 'Gattamelata'
erotic like Arabian horses and harems
but your touch
is pure electric poetry
and you become
an Italian sonnet
exclusively for me.

Stubborn Heart

My brain knows better
but my heart is a total mess.
Falling back in love
with you is a risk,
of course I know this,
but like the bungee jumper
I take the leap, the plunge,
always a chance I will land head first
perhaps paying later
with your half lies and broken promises.
The heart leads back to you;
it wants what it wants
even when it is wrong.
I would rather tremble
with passion and bursts of life—
loving you and being loved in return
so much right and perfect about that—
then play it safe.
Sure, hearts entwined could be dangerous,
but it is so fucking euphoric, liberating
when we flow in love
like a beautiful melody succinctly harmonizing,
all the cells in our bodies quivering in ecstasy.
What is the purpose of being alive
without taking a chance on love?
Danger does not intimidate me.
What frightens me most is feeling dead,
while having a pulse.

Seasonal Crush

The moon in your eyes
reflect the twilight in mine
the feel of your skin
muscles and brawn
the way you touch me instantly
with your perspicacious mind
the soft brush of your welcoming palm
from dusk until dawn
mental stimulation pouring forth
sweet like warm maple syrup
and smooth silk
the contrast
ethereal and physical
teasing all five senses
my cheeks blush like pink peonies
skin burning
flush
you have that way
that masculine gentleman touch
but with that esoteric thing going on
I might be in love
all sentimental and such
there's also a chance
it might be nothing more than a seasonal crush.

Delirious

Your lips—
sinful scarlet red,
my favorite hue of wickedly delicious!

Your skin—
a perfect painting
of pale moonlight, succulent
scent of flesh driving me
to the edge of lunacy.
I'll soon be indulging
with a bite…or two or three!

Your hair—
long and wild and raven black
and I am a clever wolf,
ravenous, ready to attack!

Otherwordly

She is psychic
a little voodoo magic
soulful
with cranberry lips
eyes full of fantastic.

Autumn

She had that autumn look in her eyes
inviting and dangerous
something about her you wanted to love
something about her a warning to run.

October

She adds a sprig of nutmeg
to her chai latte
and plays with broomsticks
and fire.
She is unruly like a black cat
on Halloween
and beautiful like autumn leaves.
It takes a strong man
to be with a woman
full of dark forests and white stars,
a woman full of all of October.

Death Lives in the Sepulcher of My Soul

You left me
crumpled love notes
strands of velvet black ink
crusty
dried
eerily like Mr. Poe
Bram Stoker, macabre
love and death
symbiotic, closely tied.

I adorned you
made you stand out
a cryptic remembrance
something almost crow-like
death-like
bloody beautiful.

I wrote you
into anomalous anthologies
a testament
to our undying, raging
peculiar love
hung you like a vampire bat
upside down
in the sepulcher of my soul
where you will forever remain
immortalized
inside my twisted poet's heart.

November

Wayward November winds
caress my bare skin
like dead flowers and silky petals of chrysanthemums,
while memories of October,
the colors of orange, red and tangerine,
float somewhere in the atmosphere
playing hide-and-seek inside my dreams.

Autumn, Almost Winter

It's autumn, almost winter
the sky a mix of hazy blue and cloudy grey

Deciduous trees are ballerinas
in the wind, their leaves fall gracefully

As I reminisce, sit and pray
a chill lingers in the air

I should be wearing sleeves
and sipping on warm apple cider

This season, how it never fails
flirting with my emotions

Reminds me of when we foreplayed outside
tumbling on top of each other

Your hand sneaking under
my little school dress
getting me hot inside the cold

Disheveled hair and stolen kisses
we broke all those stupid rules
always late for school

Taboo was our voracious love
young and fearless

All of this when I fell in love with you
in the month of November
autumn, almost winter.

Spellbound

I hope you don't mind
if I fall under your spell
there is only so much restraint
a mad girl can quell
the mystique of you
like the ghost orchid of Cuba
hauntingly beautiful and extremely rare
pulls me into you
like the tide pulls in the moon.

Your beguiling soul
and devilish grin
tantalize me, every inch
of my flesh to my core
like a quiet forest I wish to get lost in.

You are a dark flame
beautiful nocturnal animal
everything I desire and more
I am slithering down
with you
like a sleek serpentine
straight into hell.

Savage

He was a savage
a handsome hot-blooded
brute irrationally
in love with me
my Oliver, I, his Constance
Lady Chatterley's Lover.

He loved me lasciviously
yet truly and deeply
James Joyce to Nora B
maybe not your cup of tea
but he was my perfect blend
of masculine poetic sensuality.

I was besotted
with his barbaric raw intensity
the way he reached inside
grabbed my soul
setting my heart ablaze.

He filled my void
and healed an emptiness
deep within
every time we touched
stars sang in unison
the sky lit up and life
seemed all the brighter.

He watered my soul

with love and attention
respect and adoration
he nourished my mind
with intellectual stimulation
metaphysical discussions...
debates took us
all over the fucking place.

He permeated my heart
with his adoring love
he fed my body
with his body
he doused my wanting desperate lips
my aching skin
with sonnets and erotic intimacy
I called him Henry
He called me Anais.

He was a maniac utterly devoted
to loving me, and I loved him
in return, unapologetically.

Holiday

It may seem illogical
this offbeat love affair
but until I am in his rugged arms
wrapped in his strong embrace
indulging in his candy kisses
consumed in his undying love
than it all makes sense
such perfect sense.
He is my favorite holiday.
One of these days, I pray
I will open him daily—
Christmas tinsel every morning
champagne bubbles every night.
He is the sun melting the snow in my heart.

December

December is magic on my fingertips
people happy in the streets, everywhere
cheery, upbeat
I dig these vibes, warmth in the middle of winter
this month like Red Velvet cake
festive and sweet
candy canes line up sidewalks
wreaths in windows everywhere
make me feel regal, if only for this month
…and when you smile at me
I light up like Tinsel Town on Christmas Eve
my cheeks blush like Rudolph's red nose
I am melting like warm buttered caramel
December is a magic I wish we felt all year.

*Oh come
all ye misfits,
you belong
in my fun freak world.*

Insanity Invades Like a Tumor

Winter catches my long, ravishing hair
raven-black, cascading freely down my back
twisting curls into tight, painful knots
gripping my head, squeezing my skull
as autumn dissipates into the atmosphere
snow aggravates the warmth in my bones
solitude interrupts noises
whirling, swishing
inside my fragile brain
darkness dancing, laughing
invading everywhere
tormenting my head again
like a cat's midnight meow
a snake's piercing hiss
in the middle of the night
rousing the purity of my dreams
out the window I gaze, the devil's stare
gone is the sweet silence
a shrill, an ear-piercing high pitch
the top of my lungs do I scream, I scream, I scream
flirting with madness
it is cold here, wet and hard like ice
my pale skin shivers
without you here I cannot bare
I fear, I fear insanity is near
hurry, hurry you must return home…to me
so I may collapse into your arms
and you will kiss me until the chaos leaves
tease me. Intoxicate me. Take me.

Love me endless, love me crazy
until eternity, or until I die
whichever comes first.

Blue Blood Moon

The moon was aglow
blue blood and bright
ripe for lovers in love
splendid this night
legs entwined
bodies wrapped together
like two birthday gifts
tangled
between wrinkled sheets
amorous heat
planets colliding
flurry of flames
bursting like Fourth of July in our hearts
leading you home to me.

Chapter V

Wisteria

Wisteria speaks of love lost, but also of the ability for the heart to endure in spite of rejection. An incredibly durable vine, wisteria is able to live, even flourish, through mistreatment and harsh conditions.

We see more duality in love symbolism from the Victorian era, in which the language of flowers was quite intricate. The symbolism of wisteria in this age dealt a warning of clinging love and understanding that love is the fruit, but our obsession with it will be as choking as the vine.

∾ Google

Beekeeper

I must have been a beekeeper
in a past life.
I tend to fall in love
with things that sting.

Careless

You pick the most exquisite,
ornate flowers, vibrant, healthy,
full of life, watered by gentle rain,
perfumed by the sun and elemental love,
then pull delicate petals apart
with careless abandon,
no concern for their well-being.
You do the same, my love,
with my head and my heart.
Maturity and experience have taught me well...
Broken hearts make beautiful wings.

Growth

When it got really uncomfortable, when the path seemed bumpy, discordant, when situations began feeling inharmonious, forcing me to step back and analyze my life, that's when I knew real growth was occurring. Being comfortable for too long is not a positive sign— this is what people have a difficult time understanding. Stagnation is not growth, nor is it peaceful. My spirit demanded expansion, not complacency; that involved discomfort, but the end result was a remarkable place of harmony, of beauty, much like a caterpillar, transforming into an effervescent butterfly.

Necessities

I desire the night's stillness
to know the luminescence
and vibrancy of my inner light.
I crave the moon's solitude
to feel the sacredness of the sun.
I need to collapse into your arms
and sink into your kiss
to taste the magnitude of your love.

Storms

I like storms—
they energize and restore
my thirsty soul,
thinking yours will intimidate me
is where you have me all wrong.
Storms in life are necessary
for cleansing and growth.
Occasionally storms destroy,
but they also serve to make nature,
love, and people strong. And I am
inspired by the strength of broken people.
I am encouraged by their bravery.
I am in awe of their gentleness,
despite what life throws their way.
Think again before you judge,
before you assume,
to me storms are natures
way of showing us beautiful hearts
make things right; they repair and heal.

Judge me and I will understand how you view yourself.

Exuberant Introvert

I would rather dance
alone under the stars
than spend a lifetime
hiding behind the moon.

Ivy and Vine

She wears the sky like a silk robe
This nymph child, this forest queen
Branches wrap around her pristine skin
Like jewels and royalty
As if she owns the wild
She is the ivy and the vine
Poison and holy water
Fire and purity
Connected to Mother Earth
Like hummingbirds and fireflies
Freedom has found her prismatic wings
And turned her into nocturnal prose, sonnets, and poetry.

I Am

I am a raven, a witch, an angel. I fly to the sound of my heartbeat. Mother Goddess is my guide. The Universe, my voice. Like a dark magician, I am awakened to love's mystical completion. Beautifully sublime.

Anchor Me in Blood and Ink

Writing became my anchor,
my solace, my opiate of choice.
When I attempted to walk away
from my personal soul catharsis,
I felt my lungs inflate.
I found it hard to breathe.
I got the shakes and horrible headaches.
There was no peace without keyboard,
paper and pen,
only disorder, palpitations, panic.
No place to rest my scattered thoughts.
I had to write. I had to purge.
I had no other choice.

When the world is too much, create your own.
I do it every day.

"Anonymous Was a Woman"
~ Virginia Woolf

If a writer is restricted in writing,
then, surely, she is not free.
Don't try repressing the artists' message simply
because you cannot handle the sharp claws
scripted in blood and ink.

Writers cannot be silenced.
The woman born to write
will not be ensnared into quiescence.
She will not stop until her stories
dance copiously on pages
until writing liberates her completely.
And, then, she will write more
as volcanoes erupt
lava flowing
spilling inside the deep chambers
of her soul.

Fetish

I could have been any one. I could have been no one
I could have been a hero. I could have been famous
I could have been a dictator or a spectator
a lawyer, a lover
an academician, a doctor
a fiction writer, a sensual muse
a piano player singing the blues
dominatrix mistress submissive
maybe I was all of the above, maybe I was none.

One thing I certainly was
a mischievous girl
curious, cerebral
with unusual needs
blue black purple ink made me weak
in the knees
sonnets and rhymes
pulsed through my veins
like flashes of lightning and tropical rains
haikus and hymns
nimble in my brain
penetrating my core.

Catchy words, limericks, poetic adverbs
combined with a fertile imagination
twisting, gripping
growing as hydrangea on a trellis
quickly became a peculiar poetry fetish.

Always a book in hand
ideas transforming into allegories
alive and captive
between the bars of my ribs
stroking my heart
literary affairs
stories growing like grapes on a vine.

Obsessed with romance, gallantry, chivalry
old fashioned love, agape love
erotica and all of the above, this I was
a manic case of lovers becoming muses
muses becoming lovers
turning neurosis into inspiration and storybook art.

Like a voluptuous woman
a thriving citrus grove
my imagination grew as words flowed
in my inebriated reverie
like running water
hydrating my mind
I could have been anything
instead I was everything
through writing and prose, anything goes.
I was a strange girl with a peculiar poetry fetish.

A girl full of metaphors, similes, blood and ink
limericks and sonnets made me dizzy
like falling in love
I could have been anything and everything
instead, I became the fetish.

Remind Me

If I should get lost
in all the chaos
of the world,
pull out your firefly net
and catch me in the beauty
of your tender love.
Remind me of important things—
friends, flowers,
fields of cool grass
under bare feet,
blue skies above,
rain on my face,
and freedom—
freedom to make a difference,
freedom to be me.
Pull out your firefly net,
remind me of these angelic things,
and most of all, remind me
of your undying love.

Explosive Art

Art is alive, it is euphoric.
Art is ecstasy!
Proof—
You are here, breathing next to me
brewing colossal forces inside me.
I am bursting with burgundies
flurries of blue violets
lavish bright hues, kaleidoscopes, pastels.
Hymns harmonize in my head, rhapsodies when we touch.
My porcelain skin is your canvas, I am your masterpiece.
Art is anything but dead
because you are here, loving me,
despite all my imperfections
you let me love you in return.
Art doesn't get more explosive than that.

Artists contemplate the impossible and achieve madness.
We have a natural inclination to love and dream over
the edge. This is our blessing. This is our curse. Our
heaven, our hell.

Yearning

Please let me know if
I have missed any spots,
because my soul yearns
to know all of you,
each and every part.
I want your naked soul
or nothing at all.

Songbird of the Soul

I made him the hero in my story
and the center of my life.
Can you believe…I made the fiend heroic?
If that is not love, I don't know what is.

But if there is one thing I have learned
it is that poetry revives old flames and
memories cannot simply be extinguished,
and like the story that becomes indestructible
through the mere act of writing,
through bleeding tears and ink, love, too,
is an immortal songbird of the soul.

Departure

Sometimes you must let people go because their pieces no longer fit. This departure is for the betterment of your energy, your space and your precious life.

For example, when someone's main desire is to build their ego, while you are busy working on your soul the result is disharmony. The collaboration of ego and soul causes discord and strife, stifling your own personal evolvement. There are a multitude of reasons for the necessary removal of people from your life, if the dynamic of relationship no longer works no matter how many attempts to make it so.

You know in your heart if a relationship is toxic, choking the life from you. Be free of guilt attached to letting go. Learn to accept that some people are not meant to be forever in your sacred space, that this outgrowth is natural in your life's progression.

The ones you are removing served a purpose, and for that you and they are blessed, but their time in your life, and yours in theirs, has expired. Keeping toxic relationships alive only hurts you, much of the time, even the other person. Sever unhealthy ties without reproach or guilt, smile and continue on your life's journey.

Slow Down

Don't be so eager to arrive at your destination.
Take the long way. Enjoy the ride, the view.
Get a little lost, make new friends
and a few mistakes along the way.
Don't be in such a hurry to get it all right.
Future failures equal future growth.
You will have stories to share
songs to sing
art to sculpt
poetry to write
life to live
love to give.
Do not be in a hurry.
Life is too short to rush right through.

Index

Acknowledgements

To my family, thank you for putting up with me while I retreat to my girl cave to explore my mind and write with mad abandon. It is not always easy living with a writer, and I am grateful for your love and devotion, even when I demand solitude and silence. These words are for you.

To Dave, thank you for making coffee and adding your heart-made love drops. Thank you for walking with me under the stars and the moon.

To Colby and Dallas, my hearts, my joys, no words can express how deep my love is for you. All I ever want is the best for you both; for you to share your handsome, contagious smiles everywhere you go, leaving light and love into this sometimes-bitter world; to be filled with love and passion; and be ridiculously happy—that is success, remember that.

To mom, never without a smile and always positive. You encourage me in ways you know not. How did I get so lucky with you? I love you.

To my friends, both online and off, thank you for loving me, being there for me, even if it's 1000 miles away, and supporting me in special ways that you do. Sheri S., my birthday twin, I've known you all my life and the fact that we've remained friends all these years is a testament to the power of love. Jill W., my #BFF, damn girl, we go all the way back to fourth grade! What an abundance of memories we've collected! I love you so much!

To my soul sisters of the ArtistAsylum, you rock. Thank you for your energy, your friendship, your encouragement, and for considering me a "sister." You are all so talented and unique and badass, and I am blessed to know each of you.

Liz Newman, thank you for our writing collaborations. Thank you for suggesting I write book reviews. I have enjoyed that project. Thank you for writing the forward to this book! I am eternally grateful!

To my muses, I am forever indebted to the Universe for our cosmic collisions.

Finally, to my readers, who continue to inspire and encourage me daily with kindness, love, humor, feedback and all the good energy you send through the cosmos. Thank you!

About the Author

M elody Lee is a word artist who weaves thoughts, fantasies and realities into a myriad of themes, from inspirational writing to darker poems. Her poetry and prose range from love and loss, to life, growth and empowerment, written with a bohemian flair, inspired by nature, freedom and relationships. Hence, her new collection of poems, titled *Vine*, where fairytale and erotica also entwine throughout her work. Melody continues to evolve with her writing, "testing the literary waters" and exploring various genres, but mostly, you will find strong messages of empowerment, for both men and women, in her latest book, *Vine*.

Melody Lee's first book of poetry and prose, *Moon Gypsy*, has been a worldwide success, receiving rave reviews, and can be found on Amazon and other online booksellers.

Melody writes for various online magazines, including A Better Media Today and Her Heart Poetry where she reviews poetry books. She has featured some of her more edgy poetry on Creative Talents Unleashed, an online poetry blog.

You can find Melody Lee on Instagram, Facebook and Twitter at @melodyleepoetry.